PRIVATE LESSONS

THE MUSICIAN'S GUIDE TO
RECORDING

Acoustic Guitar

by Dallan Beck

ISBN 0-634-01519-2

7777 W. BLUEMOUND RD. P.O. BOX 13819 MILWAUKEE, WI 53213

Visit Hal Leonard Online at
www.halleonard.com

TABLE OF CONTENTS

4   **INTRODUCTION**

5   **QUICK GUIDE**

10   **CHAPTER 1: MIKING/DIRECT RECORDING**

17   **CHAPTER 2: LEVELS TO TAPE**

19   **CHAPTER 3: EQUALIZATION**

22   **CHAPTER 4: COMPRESSION**

25   **CHAPTER 5: RECORDING TECHNIQUES**

27   **CHAPTER 6: EFFECTS**

31   **CLOSING**

31   **ACKNOWLEDGMENTS**

Introduction

Recording acoustic guitar is sometimes viewed as a daunting task, especially for the home recording artist. Today, with more and more guitarists obtaining tabletop digital recording machines, the need to produce great-sounding acoustic guitar sounds at home is greater than ever. *Recording Acoustic Guitar* guides you on your way to making your acoustic guitar recordings sound cleaner, bigger, and better than ever—all with less time and effort.

Before we get started, you'll need a few requisite items: an acoustic guitar, a mixing board, a multitrack recorder, and a monitor system (speakers and headphones). If you have a digital multitrack recorder with a built-in mixer or a computer with digital audio capabilities, you can substitute these for traditional analog recorders and mixers.

Once you're ready to record, I strongly recommend using a microphone, compressor, and some type of effects unit (chorus, delay, reverb). It's also a good idea to have at least one CD with an example of the acoustic guitar sound you're hearing in your head (or close to it) to serve as a reference. You'll use this to gauge your progress. And yes, it will take some time and experimentation to get those great sounds, but that learning process is half the fun.

Quick Guide to Recording

The following section is a step-by-step guide to how I get acoustic guitar sounds for strumming, fingerpicking, and direct recording. One of the quickest ways to learn is to start with someone else's ideas and expand upon their information. So, if you like my sounds, feel free to use my techniques and tweak them to your ear's content.

Because sound quality is basically a matter of opinion, I want you to be able to create your own unique sounds. For this reason, Chapters 1–6 describe in great detail other recording options designed to steer you toward achieving a great acoustic guitar sound. Consider those chapters to be your reference section in case you don't thoroughly understand any of the general steps or you wish to take those general steps a bit further. Happy recording...

Strumming Guitar Parts

Step 1: Find a quiet place to record—isolated from outside noise. For this example, I'm using a condenser microphone, which is very sensitive to loud and soft sounds. For this reason, you need to find a place that doesn't have any unwanted sounds leaking into your recording environment.

Step 2: Get the guitar into a fixed position. This is usually achieved by sitting down and holding fairly still. Try to avoid extraneous movement as much as possible. Make sure that you are in tune, and if possible, have newer strings on your guitar. Remember that newer strings are more stable for tuning and have better sustain. I've also found that heavier gauge strings (I'm using .012-gauge Dean Markley strings) have a fuller, richer quality.

Step 3: Position the microphone about nine inches away from the middle of the guitar (See picture below). Nine inches is roughly the distance from my thumb to my pinky when stretched, and the middle of the guitar is where the neck meets the body (neck joint). This position is the most balanced for average guitars. However, if the guitar is too small-sounding, move it more toward the body. If the guitar is too "boomy" (like jumbo guitars can be), move it toward the fretboard or headstock. You won't know how the guitar will sound until you complete a few more steps, so you may need to change the mic position later.

Step 4: Connect your microphone to your mixer/mic preamp using an XLR cable. This allows you to use phantom power for the microphone. Using your tape machine meters as a guide, play the guitar part you are going to record (over and over) until you set proper levels to tape.

Step 5: Record the guitar part so you can listen to it and judge the basic quality of the guitar. This is a flat sound. My flat sound is on the enclosed CD as example #1. Adjust the microphone position if necessary to get a better sound. Chapter 1 on miking techniques will help you understand how moving the microphone affects the sound. You can use ex. #1 as a reference to gauge your sound quality. Repeat step 5 until you're satisfied with the raw sound of the guitar. Remember, we still have a lot of processing to do, so don't expect too much from a flat guitar sound.

Step 6: After I get a good flat sound, the next thing I do is remove unwanted frequencies from my sound. I think of it as cleaning the dishes before putting food on them. I use the EQ built into my board, but you could also hook up an external EQ on the insert path of your mixer. The frequency that bothers me the most in dreadnought or jumbo acoustic guitars is in the low-mid range. Using a normal bandwidth (Q=1.5), I cut nine decibels (db) of 250 Hz in example #2, but this can vary between 200 and 400 Hz from guitar to guitar. The reason for this is the "muddiness" associated with this frequency. The low notes often ring out of control and "mud up" the other frequencies.

Step 7: The next thing I adjust is the attack of the sound. Because I want to "soften" the strumming sound of this part, I'm going to remove 6 db at 6 kHz (Ex. #3), and my bandwidth is a little narrower (Q=2). Now the string sound is softer, and so is the attack. Because guitars vary, I've also tried removing 6 db at 3 kHz with the bandwidth still at Q=2 (Ex. #4). Notice how there is still less attack, but the strings and finger sounds are more pronounced, and the body of the guitar starts to get a little softer in volume. You may have to choose a frequency between 2 and 7 kHz to soften the sound of your particular guitar if you so desire.

Step 8: Now, it's time to start adding a few things into the mix. To keep the guitar from getting too dull, I added 6 db at 10 kHz with the bandwidth set wide at Q=1 (Ex. #5). If possible, use the EQ "shelf" button to boost all frequencies above 10 kHz, which is what I did. I understand that you may be at the mercy of your EQ's abilities, so I'm trying to pick frequencies that you should be able to come very close to. In order to add sparkle to your guitar, you may have to boost anywhere from 10 to 15 kHz.

Step 9: Look at your tape machine levels again. You may need to boost your level of recording to tape because we've taken out some loud frequencies, and you should have some room on your meters to boost the signal.

Step 10: I like to round out the whole guitar part by putting a compressor in the signal path. Place your compressor before the tape machine but after the EQ. You can use a post-EQ insert or a group output from your mixer. You could also just plug the compressor in before the cables that connect to your tape machine.

The compressor allows you to "magnify" the sound, getting it bigger and fuller to tape. All of the harmonic overtones of the instrument are raised during this process. Also, any annoying peaks on the part of the guitar player are smoothed out. I'm using a fast attack/fast release setting with a ratio of 8:1. The bottom line is the amount of reduction, and I'm using a consistent 5 db (Ex. #6). You may need to use as much as 20 db, or as little as 3 db. It depends on how much it varies on the tape machine meters. Mine varied about 10 db before compression, and I opted to cut that in half by adding 5 db of compression.

After you compress the sound, make sure you adjust the output level on the unit. If you used 5 db of reduction, you can add 5 db of output to make up for it. This way, the maximum peak doesn't change, but the overall levels underneath it are boosted.

Step 11: Record the guitar part. If you want to use effects for the purpose of making a more pleasing headphone mix, that's cool. But you should not record the effects on the same track as the dry guitar sound. Rather, you should add effects around the guitar sound—not on it. This provides you with the ability to change them at any time during the mix. To be fair, I understand that you might "have" to record your effects. Just be prepared to re-record as many times as needed to get things right.

Step 12: Options. With this type of guitar part, try adding a small room reverb (Ex. #7). I've mixed the reverb level louder than normal so you can hear the parameter settings. Decay is set to 700 ms, predelay at 10 ms, and HFC at 1 kHz. If you don't understand these parameters, read the section in Chapter 6 on reverb settings.

You could also try a chorus effect. Ex. #8 uses a chorus effect with a speed of 10% and a depth of 20% on the left side; the original sound is on the right. Ex. #9 uses reverb and chorus together.

Ex. #10 uses stereo delay as a replacement for doubling the guitar part. Some parts are too difficult to double track, or you may not have the available tracks on your recording machine for it. A short delay produces a big, wide sound to simulate a second guitar recording. The settings in my example are 19 ms for time, 0 for feedback, and 100% output.

Ex. #11 demonstrates the difference between a guitar part with stereo delay and a guitar that has been plugged into two channels and panned left and right. The example repeats itself 4 times. The first and third times are just two channels of the guitar part. During the second and fourth times, I've turned on the stereo delay. Notice how the sound "expands" when the delay is on. Try using this widening effect in one of your songs.

To add some depth to this type of wide effect, combine the stereo delay and the reverb (Ex.#12). In fact, feel free to combine any of the above mentioned effects to help you achieve the sound you're listening for.

Fingerpicking Guitar Parts

Fingerstyle guitar has its own set of quirks when it comes to recording, but there are some similarities. In this section, I used the same room in which I recorded the strumming examples. I also used the same mic placement. The first thing you should do is repeat steps 1 through 5 of the previous section to get your flat sound (Ex. #13).

Next, we need to EQ the flat sound. In Ex. #14, I cut 9 db of 250 Hz with Q=1 to remove unwanted low-mid frequencies. I then added 6 db at 7 kHz with a wide bandwidth of Q=.5 (Ex. #15). This helps prevent the finger and string sound from getting lost in the mix.

For the fingerpicking part, I used a shelf bandwidth to add 6 db at 10 kHz (Ex. #16) *instead* of adding 7 kHz. If you don't need the part to cut through, but just want it to sound bright and "bell-like," try using this setting. Of course, this all depends on your preferences.

Now we can start adding compression and effects. I used a higher ratio (12:1) with a consistent 7 db of reduction in Ex. #17 to smooth out the sound and remove annoying peaks. In Ex. #18, I chose a very small room reverb sound with the predelay at 12 ms and the decay set to 200 ms. Alternatively or additionally, you can add chorus (Ex. #19). I used the same settings as in Ex. #8. Finally, try some stereo delay (same settings as #10) to widen the panning spectrum (Ex. #20).

Direct Guitar Parts

Recording guitar parts direct removes the "hassles" of miking your instrument, but it also produces a vastly different sound. To record direct, you need to have a pickup mounted on or in your guitar. The most common acoustic guitar pickup is the piezo pickup, which converts vibrations in the guitar to an electrical signal sent through the cable to an amplification or recording device. This recording method gives you yet another option in finding the right acoustic guitar sound for you. Following are the steps for recording direct.

Using a 1/4" cable (guitar cable), plug your acoustic pickup directly into your mixer. You can hear the flat sound of my guitar direct through the mixer via a *piezo* pickup on Ex. #21. One of the first things you'll want to do is remove unwanted palm noise and low-end boom (Ex. #22). To do this, I rolled off all the frequencies below 200 Hz at a rate of 6 db per octave. Some EQs have filters that remove low-end frequencies. If your EQ has this feature, turn the knob until it reaches 200 Hz. If you don't have a shelf option, you'll need to turn the low frequency knob to around 200 Hz with a wide bandwidth, then listen and adjust until the "boomy" sound is gone.

Recording direct introduces a new source of muddiness that you'll have to deal with. In Ex. #23, I cut 9 db of 800 Hz with Q=2. This frequency often muffles the direct sound, so this adjustment helps it become a little clearer to the ears. To brighten the sound further without being piercing, try boosting 10 kHz at 6 db with a shelf for bandwidth (Ex. #24).

As with recording via a microphone, a compressor helps to fill out the sound when recording direct. In Ex. #25, I use a low ratio (3:1) with a maximum reduction of 10 db. This time, I put the compressor before the EQ but after the filter in the signal chain. If you can move the placement of the compressor in the signal path, try using it both before and after the EQ and decide where you'd like it for your sound. I'd like to explain the difference in those two positions, but that's a topic for an entire new book.

At this point in setting my acoustic sound for direct recording, I felt that the low-mid resonance was still too much, due to the placement of my compressor and the nature of recording direct. Even though I'd filtered frequencies around 200 Hz, I removed 6 db of 250hz with a Q=1 for Ex. #26. This setting removed the "rumbling" sound I was hearing from the compressor.

Next, I added some reverb to the mix. I want you to hear the difference between a darker- and brighter-sounding reverb, so Ex. #27 is a small hall reverb with 700 ms of decay, predelay at 16 ms, and HFC at 1 kHz. Ex. #28 has the same settings except for the HFC. A darker reverb will provide a more subtle effect. A brighter reverb with no high cut-off allows you to hear the finger noise and other "after sounds" of reverb. You'll have to make the choice for yourself.

To continue with effects, Ex. #29 uses a chorus effect with the speed set at 10% and the depth at 8% in the left channel and the original sound in the right. Then, in Ex. #30, I added a stereo delay with the time set at 25 ms and the feedback at 0%. You can widen the effect by setting the time at a higher value, but if it sounds out of time or just plain late, you'll need to adjust it back downward.

Miking Techniques and Direct Recording

Miking Techniques

There are two types of microphones readily available to consumers (that's you): dynamic and condenser. I recommend using condenser microphones for recording acoustic guitar. They're more sensitive than dynamic mics, allowing you to record more of your guitar's character. If you already own a condenser mic, great. If not, you may be wondering how to choose a condenser mic and/or how much to pay for one. Budget is always a concern, but remember the old saying: you get what you pay for. I recommend that your microphone be no less than half the value of your guitar. However, if your guitar cost under $100 or over $5,000, you're an exception to my little rule. In that case, buy whatever your budget allows. To help get you on the right path, I recommend the Shure KSM32 because its frequency response is well-suited for acoustic guitar and its cost is very reasonable. In fact, I used the Shure KSM32 for the music examples on the accompanying CD.

Since mic placement depends on your personal opinion of great sounds, let your ears be your guide. For each mic placement I discuss, there's an audio example on the CD (labeled by track). Try them all with your own gear and choose the position that sounds best to your ears.

So how does mic placement make such a difference in sound? Instead of giving you a bunch of frequencies and formulas that could hurt your ability to have children later, I'm going to make this clear and easy: The actual pieces of the guitar produce the sounds you are hearing. Nothing new there. The object is to figure out what each part does, what it sounds like, and where to put the microphone to get the desired blend. The closer you put the microphone to a part, the more exaggerated the response. The more you move the mic away from a part, the response is less exaggerated and contains more of a blend from the entire recording environment. Unless you're recording in an acoustically tuned environment (if you don't know what that is, then you aren't in one!) be careful of involving the room. I'm not saying, "Don't do it." I'm just saying that there are sound-affecting variables involved with each individual room that I can't even begin to imagine much less discuss in this book.

Regardless of which part(s) of the guitar you decide to mic, you also need to consider how far from that particular part you should place the mic. I'm using the distance from my thumb to my pinky (about nine inches) when my hand is stretched out. This distance keeps the guitar from having too much proximity effect. *Proximity* is when the guitar sound has an exaggerated low-end frequency response. This is normally not a very desirable effect. Think about it: When you're playing your guitar, your ears are at least twelve inches away from the instrument. The microphone acts like your ears. If I put my ear two inches away from the guitar and play, it sounds different. It's most *natural* sounding about two feet away.

So why not put the microphone by your ear? Well, first of all we need a strong signal to record to tape. Using distance miking (two feet or more) requires an acoustically proven room as well as lots of gain from the mic preamp. I use this technique in the studio as a blend quite often but only under strict isolation. When the mic preamp is turned up loud enough, the mic picks up all kinds of sound in the room, often including the room next to it, too! Also, when the mic moves farther away from the signal, we lose frequencies that are essential to the richness of the instrument. Depending on the projection of sound from your guitar, you may need to move the mic closer or farther away. Without the benefit of a spectrum analyzer, you might feel confused about where to place the mic, but there is a simple test. If the A string or low E string ring louder than the rest of the open strings, you're probably too close to the guitar, so back away a little. Unless you are too close to the soundhole, this should cure your proximity problems. Feel free to experiment with mic distances now that I've explained the precautions.

Now, we can discuss the specific sections of the guitar that can be miked. I break down the mic area into three big parts: body, neck, and headstock. Let's start with the body. The body of the acoustic guitar carries the bass response, warmth, boominess, depth, woody characteristics, power...the list goes on and on. Get the idea? There are two main parts of the body you need to be concerned with for miking purposes: the soundhole and the wood top.

Placing the microphone closer to the sound hole creates more bass response than any other place on the guitar (Ex.#31). If you have a small-body guitar, this placement helps add a fuller sound. Jumbo guitars tend to have a bit more bass response and don't need as much help from this area. If it's a bit too "boomy," try to balance it with the other guitar pieces.

As you move the microphone away from the sound hole towards the wood grain surface, the boominess goes away and is replaced by a smoother, low-midrange response (Ex.#32), though it will vary depending on the type of guitar. The sound of the wood (maple, rosewood, cardboard, etc.) resonates here. Good woods tend to please this mic placement; cheap woods do not. In this mic position, you might also start hearing the sound of the pick (if being used) or fingers of the right hand.

Now, let's experiment with mic placements around the neck. Miking the neck area creates the midrange response. This sounds more clear, cutting, jangly, and distinct. The neck joint is one of my favorite mic placements for overall balance (Ex.#33). It's close to the body, so it picks up some of the sound hole/top grain and blends in the sound of the neck.

When the mic is placed around the seventh fret, the neck sound responds with a clear sound (Ex.#34). You can hear the left-hand movement, and there's nothing to "muddy" the chord that's being played. Bigger guitars sound good with this mic position.

Finally, you can also mic an acoustic guitar near the headstock. When you place the mic at the headstock, near the nut, you pick up the sound of the strings without the interference of the guitar (Ex. #35). This is responsible for the brightness of the instrument. The bridge has the same effect, but you have to remember that the microphone will pick up whatever it is close to, and what's close to the bridge? Right, the soundhole... you're catching on. When the soundhole blends with the bridge, you get the low end response as well. This isn't a bad thing; it just isn't the same as the nut (which is two feet away from the sound hole).

I hear your question. "Why not put a mic at every piece?" Well, do you have three condenser mics? If not, don't despair. One mic can do the job, with some help from my friends: EQ, compression, and various recording techniques.

My favorite sounds come from dual mic placement. I like to blend the pieces for a sound that needs less help later. I'm trying to give you information you can use at your home studio, so I understand that some of you won't have access to two mics. For those of you that do, however, you should find the next few examples very helpful.

End of body, seventh fret

End of body, third fret

Headstock, soundhole

Neckjoint, Ambient (three feet or more)

When you use two microphones, you can either record each to their own tracks or blend them into one track. Ex. #36 and #37 have been blended, and I've recorded Ex. #38 and #39 panned hard left and right so you can hear what they sound like on separate tracks. Normally, I like to blend the mic sounds onto one track and then record the same part again with both mics, panning them left and right. It really depends on how important the part is in the song, and how much time and track space you have.

Now, choose one of these setups—or your own combination—and get levels to tape using this mic placement.

Direct Recording

If you absolutely cannot afford a condenser mic, you can use a pickup inside your guitar. It comes in handy when you don't have a good microphone or when you have a problem with isolation. If you've used a condenser mic before, you'll understand that it picks up even the quietest noise. For some people who are not able to record in a completely noise free area, a pickup is the first alternative.

Frankly, I believe that the acoustic guitar was meant to be just that: acoustic. Putting a pickup inside it is like miking an electric guitar without an amplifier. While it may have some cool sounds, I've always preferred to use a microphone whenever possible. I think that a pickup is great for live playing, where feedback problems and stage movement present convincing reasons not to use a microphone. I just don't believe in trying to replace a miked acoustic with a pickup sound. Using the two together, however, has interesting possibilities.

As far as setting up for direct recording, things don't get much simpler. If your mixing board has 1/4" inputs (like the output on your acoustic guitar), just get a 1/4" cable, plug it in, and you're good to go. If your mixer only has XLR inputs, you'll need to get a direct box. This box basically converts your 1/4" (unbalanced) sound to an XLR (balanced) connector while maintaining proper level matching. I've tried to use a hybrid cable that had one 1/4" end and one XLR end, but I lost a ridiculous amount of sound. So, be sure to use either a direct box or some other balance transformer.

Getting Quality Levels To Tape

Imagine your recording (digital or analog) as being a picture of the sound. The sharper or closer the image, the better quality you'll have from the start. Later when mixing the part, you'll be able to alter the sound to create stylistic preferences. The more sound that is saturating the tape machine, the better the quality. It's that easy to understand. When we record with digital gear, we get a higher resolution of frequencies to store on tape—more highs, more lows, and more mids. It's also the most accurate sound translation. Granted, that may not be the sound you're going for, but that's part of the trick—leaving yourself room to experiment in the mix.

Though I said that it was that easy to understand, it's not that easy to flawlessly do. You're going to notice that it's almost impossible to record consistently at the hottest level of your recording device (zero on digital units or +3 on analog). The level is going to be dynamic, meaning it's going to fluctuate up and down. That's a good thing. It gives your music freedom of expression. But too much of a good thing can be problematic. Too much fluctuation, and the levels go too high and distort, or they go too low and lose quality. Eventually, we'll try to minimize the amount of level change to best suit the music/song. To achieve this however, we'll have to call our friends: Mr. Compression and Mrs. EQ.

Before we do that, however, let's start by getting the best possible levels to tape. If your guitar has a pickup, just plug it in directly to your mic preamp. If you're recording with a mic, place it about nine inches away from the neck joint (or whichever mic placement you'd like to use).

Start now by adjusting the input level to your recorder until the loudest sound you are going to make is at either zero on your digital recorder or +3 on your tape machine. This is just for you to work on your ability to set great levels. Be sure to go through all of the acoustic parts until you get it right. In the studio, I've taken at least three full passes through the song to perfect levels to tape. How could it take so long? Because we're human and we change. One minute we're into the song, and the next we're relaxing. One part is strummed, the other is plucked. Levels change with our moods and attitudes. Take your time and do it right because you may not be able to change it later.

I CAN'T STRESS ENOUGH HOW IMPORTANT THIS IS!!

At every stage of the recording process, we are going to be readjusting levels. Please take level setting seriously. It is the only way you can get a fair chance at evaluating the quality of your recorded sound. Okay, enough of the basics. How about some tips on getting professional level results.

- If the parts you are playing are drastically different level-wise, record each part separately to get the best levels for each sound (pick, fingerstyle, etc.), so long as this doesn't compromise the flow of the guitar part.

- The better the player, the more control they have over the output of the acoustic guitar. I'm sorry to spell it out like this, but great players get great sounds. So stay on top of your chops.

- The better the guitar, the more balanced its output response from high end to low end. A good guitar does more than look good, its response is smooth and well-balanced. Try to work with a quality instrument and keep it well-maintained.

Equalization

It's time to start altering the sound of the instrument. You may have noticed that the guitar doesn't sound the same through your speakers as it does when you sit down and just play it. There are a number of reasons for this. One of which is that the levels of the frequencies of the instrument have changed. When the sound runs from a microphone, through a cable, through a mixing board, to a tape machine, back through the mixing board, then to a speaker system, and finally back to your ears via the air, well, let's just say a lot has changed. Even if you want to get the "natural" sound of the instrument on tape, it's going to take a bit of EQ to help recreate that original sound.

Take a look at your EQ. You will have some or all of these controls:

1. **Frequency selector.** This allows you to choose the target frequency you want to change. It's measured in cycles per second, more commonly known as hertz (Hz) or kilohertz (kHz). You may have as few as two of these controls or as many as 31, depending on the type of EQ you have. Some equalizers have fixed frequencies. Others allow you to choose the frequency by turning a knob. I've always preferred to have the choice myself, but I understand that you may not have this ability, so we'll do the best with what you have.

2. **Bandwidth selector.** This control adjusts how many frequencies around the chosen one are affected. It is measured in Q. Read on for a more detailed description.

3. **Boost or cut knob/slider.** This control allows you to choose how much of the selected frequency you will add or take away. It is measured in decibels (db). You might have dots around this control. Refer to your manual as to how many decibels each dot is worth.

The first thing to understand is how the frequencies and EQ affect the guitar sound. I have an unusual yet simple style for explaining EQ: Changing the frequencies changes the relative parts of the instrument. Remember, the tools you have to work with are the strings, the body, the fretboard, and you. What you need to do is find the frequencies that either add to or take away from each of those parts in order to get the sound you want. For example, if you want a smaller guitar sound, you might want to take away some of the body frequencies. If you want it to be brighter, you might want to add more string frequencies.

When you listened to my mic placement examples, you heard how moving the mic changes the sound. EQ is really just an electronic way to simulate mic placements with the ability to go beyond microphone limitations. The EQ spectrum is generally broken down into three ranges: high, middle, and low frequencies. We could spend years discussing each individual frequency, so I'll just cover the most usable ones for acoustic guitar specifically.

High Frequency (7 kHz–16 kHz)

The high frequency spectrum controls the string sound and the sound of the pick (if used). If you add more of this frequency range, the strings and pick become more pronounced in the mix, causing the overall sound to be brighter. (Use Ex. #36 as your flat sound for all of these examples; Ex. #40 boosts 10 kHz by 9 db with a shelf bandwidth.) If you take away these frequencies, they become less audible and darker-sounding. (Ex. #41 cuts 10 kHz by 9 db with a shelf bandwidth.)

Middle Frequency (1 kHz–7 kHz)

The midrange frequency spectrum controls the fretboard sound and the finger sounds of both the right and left hands. If you increase this range, the sound has more attack and stands out more in the mix. (Ex. #42 boosts 4 kHz by 9 db with a Q=1.5.) If you remove these frequencies, the sound has less attack and sits back in the mix. (Ex. #43 cuts 4 kHz by 9 db with a Q=2.)

Low Frequency (100 Hz–1 kHz)

The low frequency spectrum controls the body and wood response. When you boost this frequency range, the guitar becomes fuller and warmer; however, if you add too much, it becomes "boomy" or "muddy." (Ex. #44, "muddy," boosts 200 Hz by 6 db with a Q=2.) When you decrease this range, it becomes clearer and more precise, but too much causes it to sound thin and weak. (Ex. #45, "clear and thin," cuts 200 Hz by 9 db with a Q=2.)

A few words about bandwidth… Bandwidth (labeled Q) is the number of frequencies affected when boosting or cutting a particular frequency. Think of it as an umbrella. The frequency you choose sits in the center, and the bandwidth is divided evenly to both sides.

Confused? First, you need to understand that it is undesirable to boost or cut one individual frequency. We need to adjust an area surrounding that frequency. It might help if you know that the acoustic guitar has *overtones*. These are frequencies that resonate from the original note that has been played. So, although you might play an A=440hz (open fifth string), more frequencies actually resonate around that area.

The next thing to understand is how to control the bandwidth setting on your EQ. Hopefully, you are using a parametric EQ. This type of EQ has knobs instead of sliders with a control for bandwidth (usually labeled as Q). If you are using a graphic EQ, you have sliders instead of knobs and no controls for bandwidth. With a graphic EQ, you need to adjust several frequency points to create your own bandwidth. In other words, you would boost or cut more sliders next to each other to create a wider bandwidth.

With a parametric EQ, you pick the frequency, you choose the bandwidth, and you control how much to boost or cut. I understand that some of you will have a fixed high (HF) or low (LF) frequency point without a Q control. You're left with something like 10 kHz or 12 kHz for your HF and 80 Hz or 100 Hz for your LF. The HF will do nicely, but the LF may be a bit too low for acoustic guitar. In this case you'll have to use the mid frequency knob to do either the mid range or the low-mid range. You can adjust two out of three of the ranges at one time, or you could adjust the third range after it has been recorded. Where there's a will, there's a way.

About this "Q" parameter. It's a fairly simple formula to figure out, but you really don't need the mathematics at this point. Just to cut to the chase, the higher the Q number (2 or 3) the narrower the bandwidth, which means fewer frequencies are affected. The lower the Q number (.5 to 1) the wider the bandwidth, so more frequencies are affected. If you want to get into the physics detail (and that's cool), look through a textbook on EQ, but it's not essential for this lesson.

I wish I could just tell you how to set your bandwidth, but it's a matter of sonic taste. I will, however, let you hear some examples and let you know the Q used to get those results.

There is one more option with bandwidth, and that's something called a *shelf*. Unlike normal bandwidths, which take on a bell shape, a shelf boosts or cuts all frequencies above or below the target frequency. Let's pick 10 kHz. If you have a shelf switch, this will affect all frequencies above 10 kHz equally. You may have a LF shelf at 80 Hz. This would affect all frequencies below 80 Hz equally.

Think of setting EQ like seasoning with spices—too much or too little, and things can get ugly. One of the joys of recording is experimenting with your ears. Don't be afraid to boost or cut heavily (10 db or more) and listen to the results. Sometimes just changing the sound by 2 db doesn't produce a noticeable effect. If it sounds good to you, that's the best you can do.

Compression

Okay, it's time to put the final recorded touches on your sound. To do this, let's bring our friend Mr. Compression in to help us out. Basically, compression serves one main purpose: to keep the sound levels more consistent. Most people ignore this amazing fact. Why is it amazing? Because of the result it produces: *fuller recorded sounds* (compare Ex. #48 to Ex. #1).

The more sound you can get to tape, the thicker the result. Compression brings down your peaks so you can boost the overall recording level. This is not the same as simply making the sound louder. "Fuller" translates to more balanced frequencies. Think quality. Louder means just more of the same frequencies you're already hearing. Think quantity.

The trick is to decide how to compress your sound. Let your ears be your guide. I find myself recording the part at first just to listen to how it will sit in the mix. Are parts getting lost during the song? If so, the levels aren't consistently hot enough. Is a part losing its dynamic impact? If so, there's too much compression. Acoustic guitar fills many different needs in music. Sometimes it's a tight layer to enhance other parts. Sometimes it's a dynamic strumming or fingerpicking part to make or break the song's mood. Other times it's the only instrument in the entire mix besides the vocals.

Don't let the sound of compression scare you. I've always tried the idea in the context of the song first, before deciding yes or no. When you *hear* how compression affects the frequencies, and how it makes different sounds fit together, you'll start to understand how important it really is.

Threshold

Threshold is simply the level at which the compressor starts working. All input sounds that are below this level get passed through the unit without change, while the levels above the threshold get "compressed" according to the next few features. So you see—the compressor does not affect softer levels but instead reacts to the peaks.

Ratio

Every standard compressor has a button or knob to set the compression ratio. Basically, it compares the decibels (db) of signal above the threshold to the amount coming out of the compressor. A compressor doesn't stop all of the sound from coming out. It's not a brick wall; it *breathes*. For example, I'll explain a 3:1 ratio. For every three decibels above the threshold, one gets through the compressor. What happens to the other two? Well, they get compressed! So, if your acoustic guitar is 6 db above the threshold, 2 db of sound pass through, and 4 db get compressed.

Please don't get caught up in the math. All you need to do is look for a meter labeled something like "gain change" or "gain reduction." This meter will show you the overall amount of compression being applied to your acoustic guitar.

Now, the big issue is choosing the right ratio. The general rule is that the higher the ratio, the more compression you are likely to have. It all depends on your threshold level. Low compressor ratios (e.g., 3:1) allow more sound to sneak past the compressor while higher ratios (e.g., 10:1) prevent most peaking to tape. For a smoother, softer sound, I find myself using higher ratios (10:1 up to 20:1). For sounds that need a little more bite, I use lower ratios (2:1 up to 5:1).

That said, I always consider the compressor. If I use a 3:1 ratio on a sound, I'll need to lower the threshold considerably to balance out the sound. That means a large portion of my sound is going through that unit. If the unit is not up to the task, what do you think is going to happen to my acoustic guitar sound? All of the tone is going to be "killed" by my inferior compressor. In these cases, I use a higher ratio that allows me to only compress the peak of the sound rather than the whole sound. This leaves most of the guitar intact. Conversely, I've used amazing tube or vintage compressors with low ratios just because I liked how the compressor blended its sound with my acoustic guitar.

Attack

Though not all compressors allow you to alter the attack, it's a handy feature if available. Attack time is how quickly the compressor "reacts" when it is supposed to compress. Fast attack times (1 ms or less) reduce peaking dramatically but also take all of the punch out of the instrument. This may or may not be a desirable effect. You'll have to listen for yourself.

Longer attack times allow the sound to peak even though it goes above the threshold. Why? Because there is a delay between the when the sound peaks and the compressor starts to work. This allows for punchier sounds whose peaks aren't "squashed."

Release

Most average compressors don't allow you to change the release time. If you have an above average compressor, however, this is another cool feature for shaping your sound. Release time is how long it takes for the compressor to stop reducing the peaks of your sound. A longer release time means the entire sound gets compressed, not just the peaks. A shorter release time just affects the peak, and the body of the sound is left alone.

Output/Gain Make-up

Compression is almost useless without this last feature. It's simple to use and understand. If you look at your gain change meter, it will show you how much you are reducing the peaks of your guitar sound. You are allowed to adjust the output to "make up" for this loss of signal. If you have 6 db of gain reduction, turn up the output by 6 db. This is how the track becomes fuller. The peaks have been brought down, and the overall level brought up without changing your maximum recording level. Smile, you've just been compressed.

Quick Compression Guide

Following is a simple three-step guide for using a compressor. If you skipped ahead to this section, I recommend that you read through the detailed explanation that precedes this guide.

Step 1: Choose a compression ratio. If you've read the above section on ratios, this won't be too difficult now. If you're still confused, just start with a ratio of 3:1.

Step 2: Adjust the threshold until you have the desired amount of gain reduction—the lower the threshold, the more gain reduction you'll have. How much gain reduction should you have? It depends on how dynamic your track is (the amount of fluctuation at the tape machine meters). In general, 3 to 5 db is an average start. In some of my examples, I used up to 20 db. The better the compressor, the more natural the reduction will sound.

Step 3: Turn up the output level to compensate for the gain reduction. If the gain meter shows 8 db of reduction, turn up the output accordingly. In some units, the output knob doesn't have a db reading. Usually, it will have a meter that shows input and output levels. If this is the case, adjust the output to be the same as the input. If you don't have any of these options, simply adjust the output level while looking at your multitrack's input meter. Try to get it as high as possible without going over. If you don't have an output level, the gain make-up is automatic, and you don't have to worry about it.

*If you have attack and release options you can adjust them (using the tips I mentioned above) at any time. Just remember to do Step 3 at the end of any adjustments.

Recording Techniques

Of all the devices at your disposal, the tape machine is your best tool. A good friend of mine once said that he'd rather have unlimited time in a mediocre studio, than a short time in an amazing one. What he means is that the bottom line is the performance. All of the best effects and processors won't come close to comparing with a great part played by a great player. So, lesson #1 is: always make sure the performance is the best it can be. This means that the timing has to be in the pocket, the tuning needs to be accurate, and the part has to be right for the song. I can't help you arrange your songs, but here are a few questions to help you along:

1) How is the rhythm of the guitar when listened to by itself?
2) How does the guitar part lock into the drums?
3) Do the guitar and bass parts sound good together?
4) Does the guitar interfere with the vocal or melody?
5) Is the guitar part too busy for the song?

You get the idea. The important thing is to change any part that doesn't seem to work for the song. This could be anything from simplifying a part, breaking it into two guitar parts so it's cleaner, punching in chords that need to be re-tuned, inverting chords to fit better with other parts, or any number of variations.

Now, if you've done your homework and the parts are cool, let's discuss different ways to record your part.

Doubling

If you have a part that needs to sound "bigger," I recommend recording the part twice and panning one part hard left and the other hard right (Ex. #46). This is almost like a chorus effect or a stereo delay. I say almost, but what I mean is that this is the real thing! Chorus and stereo delay are simulations of actually recording the part twice. Unlike effects, however, the stereo field is bigger because the two parts randomly delay and chorus. This keeps the listener's ears attentive and feels bigger than the effects. The downfall of doubling is in the performance. You need to be able to play the part twice with almost no timing errors. If you can pull it off though, it's a beautifully big sound.

You can also double parts that need to be "richer." To me, that means more overtones. While grabbing a 12-string guitar might be my first thought, I usually end up doubling the idea with inversions of the chords I'm using, or I may play it up or down one octave. I get a lot of use out of a capo for this idea as well. By using one of these techniques, the chords sound like they are ringing for days because the chord has more than just three notes. The guitar fills more space harmonically but not necessarily in a spatial sense like the first doubling idea. When I double with different inversions, I usually keep the original part and the inversion panned the same. Feel free, however, to try your own panning ideas.

Open Tunings

One of the greatest sounds an acoustic guitar can make is an open chord. Don't let standard tuning keep you from having that option. I've retuned just one string at a time to make the part sing. To be honest, not only did it sound better most of the time, it was easier to play because of it! This helped me really get into the parts and out of typical chord sounds on the guitar. I won't go as far as to say I was playing more piano-style chords; I just felt a freedom in hearing different combinations of notes than otherwise possible.

I'm not going to give you "standard" open tuning ideas; that would defeat the purpose. The idea is for you to analyze your parts and see where a string tuned up or down either a half or whole step would open up the possibility of using more open strings.

Dividing The Part

When I write a song, I almost always write many parts at once without realizing it. The guitar part is actually the drum, bass, and vocal parts all rolled into one. I've learned to listen to my parts and take away things that were meant for other instruments. I'm not alone in this. Almost every session I've produced has involved helping people work out the parts so they sound better in the mix. Typically, this eventually involves simplifying the part or letting other instruments take over. It's not always necessary for the acoustic part to be playing the bass line. Neither is it always cool to have the guitar strumming 100% of the time, taking away from the drummer's hi-hat groove.

However, I do like to use as much of the guitar as possible. Sometimes this means taking an awkward guitar part, or one that just sounds too muddy because of too many notes on top of each other, and dividing it into two or three little guitar parts. This makes the recording cleaner. The parts may be divided so that high notes are on one track while lower ones are on another. Or one part becomes a rhythm part while the other fills the holes.

Effects

Before I explain the types of effects and their parameters, let me first recommend that you use the effects during the mixing session. While I understand that you may want to hear effects while you are recording the guitar parts, that doesn't mean that you have to put them to tape. The idea is to have the effects connected after the multitrack. This can be done by using your mixer's auxiliary outputs, which act as external outputs to effects processors. If you don't have these, you might have group outputs. These generally go before the tape machine, but in a mix session, there's no more recording, so you can use these as extra outputs, and then use an extra fader for your effects return. Most mixing boards have more fader paths than you have tracks on your tape machine. During recording, this allows you to use one fader to set levels to tape and one fader to set levels for listening. In the mixing process, it allows you to use some of the "extra" faders for effects returns.

What I'm trying to get at is for you to have the "dry" (no effect) guitar part on one channel and the "wet" (effect) sound on another. This allows you to decide how much effect you want to use right up until the last minute of your final mixdown. This is important because effect levels sound different when you add other instruments to the mix. For example, when you listen to a reverb on a guitar by itself, it may sound like too much effect. However, once you add in the drums, bass, vocals, etc., it may become difficult to hear what the effect is supposed to be doing. So, if at all possible, please use the effects after the signal gets past the tape machine rather than before. You'll have an easier time working with the effects, and you'll maintain the ability to experiment right up until you mix down to a DAT or CD.

Reverb

Reverb simulates recording in different environments. These could be small rooms, large halls, stone chambers, concert arenas, etc. They also have different shapes, sizes, and surface materials. Depending on the abilities of your processor, you'll have a wide variety of options to choose from.

Reverb is used to add depth to a sound—give it a three-dimensional feel. If you have one sound with reverb and one without, the one with reverb will sound farther back in the speakers, while the other will sound more up front and close to you. It is also used to add a short amount of sustain to a sound, or to help fill the gaps between the notes. The trick is finding the reverb that best suits the part.

Let's start by saying that rhythmic, staccato, and fast parts usually sound better with tighter, smaller reverbs. If you have a guitar part that's strumming an important rhythm in the context of the song, room reverbs are most often the verbs of choice. This gives the part depth without muddying the rhythm. Examples of room reverbs are: small room, large room, small chamber, closet, bathroom, etc. (Ex. #7 and Ex. #18).

If you have a legato, single-note, slow, or open-sounding part, you can use a little more reverb. Hall reverbs tend to help fill in the spaces between the notes nicely. Examples of halls are: large hall, auto park, small hall, cathedral, etc. (Ex. #27 and Ex. #28).

If you are hearing (in your head) a very bright reverb, you may choose a plate reverb (Ex. #47). Plates are simulations of reflections off of a metallic surface. Be careful with bright reverbs on fast or highly rhythmic parts. Using plates on these can cause you to hear too many reflections and mess up the rhythm of the part. Examples of plates are snare plate, fat plate, thin plate, etc.

If you're lucky (or wealthy) enough to own a reverb that has adjustable parameters, let me give you some tips to using these:

Size or time or decay: This parameter allows you to lengthen (or shorten) the reverb reflections. It's measured in milliseconds (ms). I would recommend using this parameter to fit the tempo of the guitar part. Try to have the reverb last long enough to fill the gaps between the notes. Adjust the length of the reverb time using this parameter.

High frequency cut-off/low-pass filter: This parameter lets you darken the reverb by removing unwanted high end from it. If your reverb doesn't sound good to you, you might want to remove some of the high end frequencies that cause it to sound fake. This also helps "warm" a reverb that sounds too harsh. This parameter is measured in Hz or kHz. For example if you set the HFC to 10 kHz, the reverb will not have any frequencies *above* 10,000 Hertz. The lower the number, the darker the sound of the reverb will be. Attack for the guitar usually sits somewhere around 3 kHz to 5 kHz. If you set the HFC below that, (1 kHz or less) the reverb will lose its attack and soften up. If you follow my instructions, the guitar will still have its attack, but the reverb won't; this could help the reverb of a highly rhythmic part sit better in the mix.

Predelay: There may be a parameter that allows you to delay the sound of the reverb by milliseconds. This predelay is the amount of time the processor waits before letting you hear the reverb. This comes in handy when you have the right amount of reverb, but it's still muddying the guitar part. Predelay allows you to hear the sound of the guitar first, and then the reverb. Sometimes having the reverb "on top" of the sound just doesn't work.

My best analogy for using predelay is one that I think everyone can relate to. Have you ever seen a band play at a concert? If you sit in the middle of the room, you get a decent mix of reverb (from the concert hall) and the band's sound coming off the stage. The farther back you go (away from the stage), the more the band blends in with the reflections of the concert hall. This causes the band to sound unclear because the "effect" is on top of the sound. The closer you get to the stage, the less effect you hear, and the more you hear the band. The reverb of the room is delayed in getting to you because it has to travel farther from the walls to your ears. If you've ever played on a stage in a big room, it almost feels like their isn't any reverb—until you stop playing. The predelay is so long that it almost sounds like delay.

With that story out of the way, how about some setting suggestions? Zero ms of predelay gives you no delay at all. This is good for parts that are not rhythmic in context of the song. Ten to thirty ms will give the sound a little room to cut through in the mix without messing up the timing of the part. Fifty to 100 ms is a setting that could be used for a part that doesn't need much reverb except at the end. The reverb will be delayed so much that it will be all but lost while playing, but when you stop, and there is a "gap" in the part, the reverb will come through and fill it.

Chorus

Chorus is a modulation effect that slightly detunes the pitch of the guitar part. It's like recording the same part twice and having a *slight* tuning difference between the parts—and I emphasize the word slight. If the chorus has too much detune, it just sounds out of tune. This is a nice way to thicken a guitar part that you aren't going to record twice. The original guitar part gets panned to one side while the effect is put on the other side. This makes two sounds out of one and fills more space while adding a smooth texture to the part (Ex. #19 and Ex. #29). The adjustable parameters of chorus are:

Depth/Pitch change: This controls how much the pitch gets detuned. It's measured in cents. Some units don't have a measurement on the front panel, or may have a number system from 0-100. It simply varies between a little and a lot of pitch change. The more depth, the more "watery" the sound becomes until it reaches the point where it simply goes out of tune.

Rate/Speed: This controls how fast the depth range is affected. Slower speeds take longer to go through the depth setting. Faster rates take less time to get detuned and re-tuned. When the rate is very fast and the depth is minimal, it almost sounds like vibrato. Speed is measured in kilohertz. However, many units use a percentage system from 1-100, or a number system from 0-99.

Predelay: This controls the amount of time before the effect is heard. It is measured in milliseconds. The longer the time, the wider the stereo image will be, until you go too far, and it just starts to sound out of time. Standard settings start at 5 ms and can go as high as 60 ms. I find that a setting of 20-30 ms is usually appropriate to get a wide stereo image without messing up the tightness of the part.

Stereo Delay

When I'm unable to track a part a second time, I'll revert to stereo delay to get a bigger guitar sound. When the guitar part is improvised, just too hard to double, or if you've simply run out of tracks, this effect come in handy. Basically, you are simulating an exact copy of the guitar part that was recorded, only slightly delayed in time. By panning these two sounds left and right, you create a stereo image from a mono sound (Ex. #10 and Ex. #30). It differs from normal delay effects in that we will only be hearing one delay. All we want is one copy of the sound, no more.

*One word of caution. In any instance that you have two sounds from the same guitar part, you run the risk of phase cancellation. When this happens, the two parts cancel out frequencies from each other and you lose sound. This will be noticed as less low-mid bass frequencies if you have them panned in the same area. If they are panned far left and right, it will make them sound wider than where the actual speakers are! This can be a neat effect on a part that is more textural in nature within the song. As you adjust the delay time, this phase condition will change from in- to out-of-phase. Make sure you listen to the time setting you're using before deciding on using just a random number. If you're trying to make the sound bigger, phase cancellation would be your enemy. If you're trying to make it sound wider, it could be your friend. Listen with headphones as well as with speakers before deciding on an out-of-phase part. The parameters for delay are :

Time: This controls the duration of time before the effect is heard. It is measured in milliseconds. To use this as a stereo delay effect, keep the setting between 5 and 50 ms.

Feedback: This controls the number or repeats that are heard. This is measured many different ways, from a percentage to a random number from 0-99. The idea is to set this to the lowest setting, so that only one reflection is heard. Remember, we are using this to simulate an exact copy of the original part, not a Grand Canyon-like echo effect.

Closing

I hope this has been a helpful tool for you for recording acoustic guitar sounds. Re-read the different sections as many times as you wish—you never know what you'll pick up each time. Knowledge comes to those who seek it, but at its own pace. I wish you peace, patience, and passion.

— Dallan Beck

Acknowledgments

Written and engineered by: Dallan Beck

Original music by: Dallan Beck

Recorded at: Musicians Institute

Photography by: Tevis Sauer and Hila Calif

Assisted by: Susan Ostroske, RIT class of 2000

Product support from: Ryan Smith at Shure Inc., David Lienhard and Merle Saunders at Dean Markley

A special thank you to everyone at Hal Leonard Corporation

MUSICIANS INSTITUTE

Press

Musicians Institute Press

is the official series of Southern California's renowned music school, Musicians Institute. **MI** instructors, some of the finest musicians in the world, share their vast knowledge and experience with you — no matter what your current level. For guitar, bass, drums, vocals, and keyboards, **MI Press** offers the finest music curriculum for higher learning through a variety of series:

ESSENTIAL CONCEPTS
Designed from MI core curriculum programs.

MASTER CLASS
Designed from MI elective courses.

PRIVATE LESSONS
Tackle a variety of topics "one-on-one" with MI faculty instructors.

FOR MORE INFORMATION, SEE YOUR LOCAL MUSIC DEALER, OR WRITE TO:

HAL•LEONARD®
CORPORATION
7777 W. BLUEMOUND RD. P.O. BOX 13819 MILWAUKEE, WI 53213

Prices, contents, and availability subject to change without notice. Some products may not be available outside of the U.S.A.

GUITAR

Advanced Scale Concepts & Licks for Guitar
by Jean Marc Belkadi
Private Lessons
00695298 Book/CD Pack $12.95

Basic Blues Guitar
by Steve Trovato
Private Lessons
00695180 Book/CD Pack $12.95

Creative Chord Shapes
by Jamie Findlay
Private Lessons
00695172 Book/CD Pack $7.95

Diminished Scale for Guitar
by Jean Marc Belkadi
Private Lessons
00695227 Book/CD Pack $9.95

Guitar Basics
by Bruce Buckingham
Private Lessons
00695134 Book/CD Pack $14.95

Guitar Hanon
by Peter Deneff
Private Lessons
00695321 . . . . $9.95

Guitar Soloing
by Dan Gilbert & Beth Marlis
Essential Concepts
00695190 Book/CD Pack $17.95

Harmonics for Guitar
by Jamie Findlay
Private Lessons
00695169 Book/CD Pack $9.95

Jazz Guitar Chord System
by Scott Henderson
Private Lessons
00695291 . . . . $6.95

Jazz Guitar Improvisation
by Sid Jacobs
Master Class
00695128 Book/CD Pack $17.95

Modern Approach to Jazz, Rock & Fusion Guitar
by Jean Marc Belkadi
Private Lessons
00695143 Book/CD Pack $12.95

Music Reading for Guitar
by David Oakes
Essential Concepts
00695192 . . . . $16.95

Rhythm Guitar
by Bruce Buckingham & Eric Paschal
Essential Concepts
00695188 . . . . $16.95

Rock Lead Basics
by Nick Nolan & Danny Gill
Master Class
00695144 Book/CD Pack $14.95

Rock Lead Performance
by Nick Nolan & Danny Gill
Master Class
00695278 Book/CD Pack $16.95

Rock Lead Techniques
by Nick Nolan & Danny Gill
Master Class
00695146 Book/CD Pack $14.95

BASS

Arpeggios for Bass
by Dave Keif
Private Lessons
00695133 . . . . $12.95

Bass Fretboard Basics
by Paul Farnen
Essential Concepts
00695201 . . . . $12.95

Bass Playing Techniques
by Alexis Sklarevski
Essential Concepts
00695207 . . . . $14.95

Grooves for Electric Bass
by David Keif
Private Lessons
00695265 Book/CD Pack $12.95

Music Reading for Bass
by Wendy Wrehovcsik
Essential Concepts
00695203 . . . . $9.95

Odd-Meter Bassics
by Dino Monoxelos
Private Lessons
00695170 Book/CD Pack $14.95

KEYBOARD

Music Reading for Keyboard
by Larry Steelman
Essential Concepts
00695205 . . . . $12.95

R & B Soul Keyboard
by Henry J. Brewer
Private Lessons
00695327 . . . . $16.95

Salsa Hanon
by Peter Deneff
Private Lessons
00695226 . . . . $10.95

DRUM

Brazilian Coordination for Drumset
by Maria Martinez
Master Class
00695284 Book/CD Pack $14.95

Chart Reading Workbook for Drummers
by Bobby Gabriele
Private Lessons
00695129 Book/CD Pack $14.95

Working the Inner Clock for Drumset
by Phil Maturano
Private Lessons
00695127 Book/CD Pack $16.95

VOICE

Sightsinging
by Mike Campbell
Essential Concepts
00695195 . . . . $16.95

ALL INSTRUMENTS

An Approach to Jazz Improvisation
by Dave Pozzi
Private Lessons
00695135 Book/CD Pack $17.95

Encyclopedia of Reading Rhythms
by Gary Hess
Private Lessons
00695145 . . . . $19.95

Going Pro
by Kenny Kerner
Private Lessons
00695322 . . . . $19.95

Harmony & Theory
by Keith Wyatt & Carl Schroeder
Essential Concepts
00695161 . . . . $17.95

Lead Sheet Bible
by Robin Randall
Private Lessons
00695130 Book/CD Pack $19.95

WORKSHOP SERIES
Transcribed scores of the greatest songs ever!

Blues Workshop
00695137 . . . . $19.95

Classic Rock Workshop
00695136 . . . . $19.95

R & B Workshop
00695138 . . . . $19.95